THE COMEBACK

IT'S NOT TOO LATE AND YOU'RE NEVER TOO FAR

Louie Giglio

with Dixon Kinser

W PUBLISHING GROUP

AN IMPRINT OF THOMAS NELSON

Published in Nashville, Tennessee, by W Publishing, an imprint of Thomas
Nelson. W Publishing and Thomas Nelson are registered trademarks of
HarperCollins Christian Publishing, Inc.

Unless otherwise indicated, all Scripture quotations are taken from the
New International Version®, *NIV*®. Copyright © 1973, 1978, 1984, 2011 by Biblica, Inc.®
Used by permission. All rights reserved worldwide.

Thomas Nelson titles may be purchased in bulk for educational, business,
fund-raising, or sales promotional use. For information, please e-mail
SpecialMarkets@ThomasNelson.com.

ISBN 978-0-310-88738-6

August 2015 / Printed in the United States of America

CONTENTS

INTRODUCTION

They say everybody loves a comeback story. And what's not to love? A smaller, weaker, less capable underdog goes up against the bigger, stronger, more talented opponent. It seems as if the writing is on the wall and there is no way the underdog can win the contest until... something happens! The tide starts to turn in the underdog's favor. The underdog keeps the pressure on his opponent with the sheer impossibility of the circumstances fueling his determination, until... triumph! What seemed impossible has been accomplished. A contest that seemed like certain defeat has, inexplicably, turned into a victory, and the underdog has come out on top!

You can see why we love these stories. What drama! What excitement! Whether it is a sporting event, movie, or television program, we love a good underdog story because somewhere, down deep, we know it's our story too. There are a lot of things we encounter in this life that feel insurmountable. Our circumstances can feel like a bigger, stronger, more capable opponent and we, well, we feel small, weak, and hopeless. Do you know that place? If so, you are in the right place, because God has good news for you.

The *comeback* is that crucial moment in the underdog story when the tide starts to turn. It's when the momentum starts to grow until, against all odds, the underdog begins to win. However, such comebacks do not come by chance, luck, or good fortune. They come about because there is a God who is on our side and who is actively working to make them possible in our lives! Trust in this God-for-us reality is what drives this study, and it is what you will be invited to open up to during the next few weeks.

God is the God of the comeback, and if you're longing for some sort of a turnaround or fresh start or new direction, this study is for you. In the next six sessions, we will look at stories of men and women in the Bible to see how God gives hope to the hopeless, direction to the directionless, and help for those who need help. In each session, expect an opening question, a short Bible study, and some time with Louie on the video. The real action will come after the video, when you dig into each topic through a guided small group experience. During this time, your group will be invited to participate in a practical activity designed to move that session's comeback lesson from your head to your heart. This section is called "Opening Up to the Comeback," and it should serve as a place where the big ideas of *The Comeback* take on some flesh-and-blood reality.

It's going to be great! However, if you want to get the most out of your *Comeback* experience, you need to keep a couple of things in mind. First, the real growth in this study will happen during your small group time. This is where you will process the content of Louie's message, ask questions, and learn from others as you listen to what God is doing in their lives.

Second, remember that as much as small groups can be a deeply rewarding time of intimacy and friendship, they can also be a challenge. Work to make your group a "safe place." That means being honest about your own thoughts and feelings as well as listening carefully to everyone else's opinion.

Third, resist the temptation to "fix" a problem someone might be having or to correct his or her beliefs. That's not what this time is for.

Finally, keep everything your group shares confidential. All this will foster a rewarding sense of community in your *Comeback* group and give God's Spirit some space to heal, challenge, and engineer a comeback in your life.

HOW TO USE THIS GUIDE

As you'll discover, *The Comeback* is as personal as it is practical. Each session begins with an icebreaker question followed by a reflection from the Bible. You will then watch the video of Louie Giglio's message and jump into some directed small group discussion. Even though there are many questions available for your small group, don't feel like you have to use them all. Your leader will focus on the ones that resonate most with your group and guide you from there.

The final component of each session is called "Opening Up to the Comeback." This is where *The Comeback* might be unique from other studies you may have experienced. Here your group will engage in a hands-on practical exercise that seeks to move the good news of the study from the head to the heart. Think of this time as an answer to the question, "What am I supposed to *do* with this message?"

These exercises are meant to be completed during your group time, and they will be what you make of them. If you choose to only go through the motions, or if you decide to not participate, there is a lesser chance you'll find what you're looking for in this study. But if you stay open-minded and take a chance, you'll discover what so many others have already found to be true: faith comes alive when you take holy risks for God.

Now, it is understandable if the thought of "risky" activities makes you anxious. That's okay. If you fall into this category, just read ahead to each "Opening Up to the Comeback" section. This way, you will know not only what's coming but also how to prepare yourself. None of these exercises involves anything inappropriate or embarrassing. They are just hands-on opportunities for you to participate with God in the comeback he so eagerly wants for you.

Following your group time, there will be three more opportunities for you to engage with the content of *The Comeback* during the week. The first is activity-based (*Action*), the second is a Bible study (*Contemplation*), and the third is a meditation on a chapter from the book (*Reflection*). The challenge is to do at least one of these activities between sessions and to use this study guide to record what you learn. Beginning in Session 2, you will have time before the video to check in about the previous week's activity and process your experiences as a group. Don't worry if you couldn't do an activity one week or are just joining the study. Hearing what others have learned will be nourishment enough.

Remember that whatever problems you're going through, God already knows what the solutions are. No matter what kind of grief or pain or trouble or heartache you encounter, he can provide for your needs. God is in the business of giving comebacks to people, and even when things look their bleakest, they may not be that way at all. Help is at hand.

So, are you ready to receive what God has in store for you? Are you ready to start your comeback? Let's jump into *The Comeback* and begin.

IF YOU ARE A GROUP LEADER, there are additional instructions and resources in the back of the book for leading the "Opening Up to the Comeback" sections. Because some of the activities require materials and setup, make sure you read this section over so you will be prepared for each week's activity.

SESSION **1**

A DEEPER KIND OF
COMEBACK STORY

*What we're celebrating here is
the God of all the comeback stories.*

Louie Giglio

Orientation

Have you ever watched parents try to get their children to apologize to each other when it is clear neither of those children want to? It is truly painful to watch. The parents know they are doing the right thing by steering their children toward forgiveness and reconciliation, yet as the kids resist, it becomes clear the whole affair is going nowhere. Why? Because the kids are just not open to it. Sure, the parents may succeed in getting the two of them to say, "I'm sorry," but everyone knows they're just going through the motions. And true reconciliation is not possible unless both parties are willing to open up.

God is the God of the comeback. There is no dream of yours that's been dashed, mistake you have made, or tragedy you can encounter that God cannot redeem, restore, and make new. It's what God does and who he is. But even more than that, it is what God *wants* to do in your life right now. God would like nothing more than to offer you a great comeback where you need it most. But you have a part to play. Just like those kids who need to apologize to each other, you have to be open to God's work in your life.

This is often easier said than done, because when life knocks you around, it can be easy to put up barriers. Maybe you have done something foolish you are ashamed of, or maybe you made good choices but the bottom fell out on you, or maybe life just threw you a curveball and you are not sure how a good God fits into the tragedy you have suffered. These kinds of experiences can leave you feeling distant from God and unsure of what to do about it. The longer this persists, the more you can put up walls and defenses until—like the two kids being forced to apologize—you stop being open to God's best and settle for something lesser.

But here's the good news: *it doesn't have to be this way.* That is what the first session of *The Comeback* is all about. God wants to ignite a massive comeback in your life—and he is already open to doing it. The question is, *are you?* What would it take for you to be open to the comeback God wants to orchestrate? Is anything blocking your heart? If so, it's okay; just head into the session asking yourself, *What if things could really change? What if things could really be different for me tomorrow?*

God already has an answer for this question. Do you?

Welcome and Checking In

Go around the group and invite the members to introduce themselves, and then answer the following questions:

- If you had one whole day to yourself, where would you go and what would you do?

- If you could describe your hopes for this study in one word, that word would be: _____.
  Why did you answer the way you did?

Hearing the Word

Read aloud in the group the following passages from Exodus 2:11–15 and 3:1–12. Invite everyone to listen for a fresh insight during the reading.

²:¹¹ *One day, after Moses had grown up, he went out to where his own people were and watched them at their hard labor. He saw an Egyptian beating a Hebrew, one of his own people.* ¹² *Looking this way and that and seeing no one, he killed the Egyptian and hid him in the sand.* ¹³ *The next day he went out and saw two Hebrews fighting. He asked the one in the wrong, "Why are you hitting your fellow Hebrew?"*

¹⁴ *The man said, "Who made you ruler and judge over us? Are you thinking of killing me as you killed the Egyptian?" Then Moses was afraid and thought, "What I did must have become known."*

¹⁵ *When Pharaoh heard of this, he tried to kill Moses, but Moses fled from Pharaoh and went to live in Midian . . .*

³:¹ *Now Moses was tending the flock of Jethro his father-in-law, the priest of Midian, and he led the flock to the far side of the wilderness and came to Horeb, the mountain of God.* ² *There the angel of the* LORD *appeared to him in flames of fire from within a bush. Moses saw that though the bush was on fire it did not burn up.* ³ *So Moses thought, "I will go over and see this strange sight—why the bush does not burn up."*

⁴ *When the* LORD *saw that he had gone over to look, God called to him from within the bush, "Moses! Moses!"*

And Moses said, "Here I am."

⁵ *"Do not come any closer," God said. "Take off your sandals, for the place where you are standing is holy ground."* ⁶ *Then he said, "I am the God of your father, the God of Abraham, the God of Isaac and the God of Jacob." At this, Moses hid his face, because he was afraid to look at God.*

⁷ *The* LORD *said, "I have indeed seen the misery of my people in Egypt. I have heard them crying out because of their slave drivers, and I am concerned about their suffering.* ⁸ *So I have come down to rescue them from the hand of the Egyptians and to bring them up out of that land into a good and spacious land, a land flowing with milk and*

honey—the home of the Canaanites, Hittites, Amorites, Perizzites, Hivites and Jebusites. ⁹ And now the cry of the Israelites has reached me, and I have seen the way the Egyptians are oppressing them. ¹⁰ So now, go. I am sending you to Pharaoh to bring my people the Israelites out of Egypt."

¹¹ But Moses said to God, "Who am I that I should go to Pharaoh and bring the Israelites out of Egypt?"

¹² And God said, "I will be with you. And this will be the sign to you that it is I who have sent you: When you have brought the people out of Egypt, you will worship God on this mountain."

In groups of two or three, share your answers to the following questions:

What was one thing that stood out to you from the Scripture?

In what ways did that represent a new insight?

Do you think this part of the book of Exodus casts Moses in a good or bad light? Why did you answer the way you did?

Watch the Video

Play the video segment for Session 1. As you watch, use the following outline to record any thoughts or concepts that stand out to you.

Notes

All of us know what it means to be in that moment when we need God to come through for us, and all of us love to celebrate those great comeback stories when they occur.

The greatest comeback occurred when Jesus was raised up out of the grave into everlasting life. Now, we can celebrate the power of God that can bring us back even from the brink of death.

Moses was in his eighties and on the back side of nowhere, tending to his father-in-law's flocks, when he received his comeback in life.

At a time when many would be thinking about their last chapters on this earth, God spoke to Moses out of a burning bush and called him into a position of leadership.

God was able to use Moses because he submitted his life to God's plans and purposes and allowed the Lord to unfold his comeback story.

Like Moses, we may feel that we are on the back side of nowhere, or that we've done too much wrong and there is no way back. But Moses' story shows us that God sees us where we are and will find us there. He is the God who can restart the story.

Our part in this is to believe that wherever we are, God is with us and is present in our lives.

Scripture says that God "gives songs in the night" (Job 35:10). When the cloud comes, we can praise God and have a song in our heart—and he will lead us back to the land of the living.

Group Discussion

Take a few minutes with your group members to discuss what you just watched and explore these concepts in Scripture.

First Impressions

1. Before everyone shares in the large group, turn to one or two people next to you and finish this sentence: "After watching the video, one question I now have is . . . "

Community Reflection

2. Even if you have felt like you've done too much, gone too far, or God has lost track of you, the truth is God has not forgotten you. God sees you right where you are. In what ways do you agree or disagree with this statement?

3. Does this idea sound too good to be true? Why or why not?

4. Have you ever seen God restart someone's story? If so, when?

5. God can "reach into our lives and make music play." What does the "music" playing in your life sound like right now? What would God's song sound like?

6. In the video, Louie says he wished he could say his story ended with everything getting better quickly and easily . . . but it didn't. It took time. Do you find this comforting or discouraging? Why did you answer the way you did?

7. Can you think of a place in your life where you need a comeback? If so, are you willing to share with the group what that is?

Opening Up to the Comeback

For this activity, each participant will need a blank piece of paper, a pen, and an envelope.

In this session, you have explored what it means that "God is the God of the comeback." Such comebacks are dependent on the power of God to make them a reality—and all you have to do, as Louie says, is be open to them. This prayer exercise is designed to help you take steps toward becoming more open to the work God wants to do in your life.

Take a few minutes to pray, and then answer the following question on the blank piece of paper you have been given: *If God could change one thing in my life right now, what would I want that to be?* Be as honest as you can. This will go into a sealed envelope, and no one will ever see it but you.

Once you have written your answer, flip the paper over. Then, as a sign of being open to God's movement in this area of your life, write one word: "help."

Take a few minutes to pray and then fold up your paper, put it inside your envelope, seal it, and write your name on the front. Hand your envelope to your group leader, who will hold it (unopened) until the last session. Make this act of handing it over a symbolic act that reflects your desire to entrust your comeback to God.

Closing Prayer

Close the session by praying together for a couple of minutes. First, offer a one-word prayer for the concern you wrote down on your paper. Next, pray that the person on your left will be open to the power of God working in his or her life to bring about a comeback. Finally, pray that the person on your right will be able to hear God's song playing in his or her life this week.

BETWEEN-SESSIONS PERSONAL STUDY

You are invited to further explore the good news of *The Comeback* by engaging in any or all of the following between-sessions activities. Remember, this is part of *The Comeback* experience, not about following rules or doing your home-work—these activities (categorized as *Action*, *Contemplation*, and *Reflection*) are designed to give you opportunity to be open to God working out a comeback in your life. *Be sure to read the reflection questions after each activity and make a few notes in your guide about the experience.* There will be a time for you to share these reflections at the beginning of the next session.

Action: Sing!

In the video this week, Louie shares about how he found a way to connect with God during some of his darkest hours by singing to him. When he would sing, the cloud of anxiety and oppression over him would lift, prompting him to say, "God, I can't see you, but I'm going to praise you." Picking up on this promise, you are invited to do something risky and radical: engage the worry and anxiety of your life with a song. There are two paths to choose for this exercise:

1. **Actual Singing:** Write a song to God, or choose a simple one you know by heart (this could be an old hymn, a new worship song, or even something as simple as "Jesus Loves Me" from your childhood). Whenever you feel the cloud of gloom, stress, or anxiety overshadow you, begin to sing your song. You can sing it as loudly or as quietly as you like—it is up to you. Just sing it out, and see what God does next.

2. **Metaphorical Singing:** During the video, Louie mentioned that God gave him "songs in the night" (Job 35:10) that led him back into "the land of the living" (Psalm 27:13). If you are not a singer, or if you find yourself in a place where singing would not be appropriate, use Psalm 27 as your song this week. Whenever you feel the cloud of gloom, stress, or anxiety darken your path, say a portion or all of Psalm 27 out loud and see what God does next.

Make a few notes about your experience to share with the group next week.

The good news is that the life Jesus calls us all to enter is a life of come-back . . . It may be the kind of comeback where we overcome obstacles by God's power . . . [or] it may be a deeper sort of comeback, where Jesus redeems the worst of circumstances for his glory and our best.

—The Comeback, *page 6*

Contemplation: Pay Attention

For this week's contemplation, review this story of Moses and the burning bush told in Exodus 3:1–6:

> [1] *Now Moses was tending the flock of Jethro his father-in-law, the priest of Midian, and he led the flock to the far side of the wilderness and came to Horeb, the mountain of God.* [2] *There the angel of the LORD appeared to him in flames of fire from within a bush. Moses saw that though the bush was on fire it did not burn up.* [3] *So Moses thought, "I will go over and see this strange sight—why the bush does not burn up."*
>
> [4] *When the LORD saw that he had gone over to look, God called to him from within the bush, "Moses! Moses!"*
>
> *And Moses said, "Here I am."*
>
> [5] *"Do not come any closer," God said. "Take off your sandals, for the place where you are standing is holy ground."* [6] *Then he said, "I am the God of your father, the God of Abraham, the God of Isaac and the God of Jacob." At this, Moses hid his face, because he was afraid to look at God.*

There are few stories from the Bible as famous as this one. The story of Moses and the burning bush has been depicted in film, animation, oil paintings, stained glass, and statuary. It resonates with us on a deep, almost primal level. However, if we are not careful, our familiarity with the story can cause us to assume we already know what it has to say and gloss over some of its most powerful insights. We stop paying attention, and we miss some deeper truths.

Paying attention, in fact, might be one of the main points of this text. Some of the oldest interpretations of the encounter suggest that Moses and the burning bush is not a story about a miracle but about a *test*.[1] What kind of test? Good question.

Exodus 3:2 says, "Moses saw that though the bush was on fire it did not burn up." How did Moses know *that*? He could tell easily the bush was on fire, but how long did it take before he realized the fire was not consuming the bush? Well, how long would it take you? One minute? Five minutes? Ten minutes?

The point is that Moses noticed because he was paying attention. He was awake and alert enough to notice not only that the bush was on fire but also that it was not being consumed. That is where the miracle was, and that is when he heard God speak!

On a scale of 1 to 10, with 1 being slow and 10 being fast, how fast is your pace of life?

What makes it hard to notice the places that God is active around you?

What is one concrete action you could take to slow down this week in order to better notice the sacredness of the everyday?

Moses had a great comeback story over his anger and failed opportunities. But he also had a speech impediment and lousy self-confidence. He didn't think he could do anything useful for God, but along with his brother, Aaron, he went to Pharaoh and told him to let God's people go. Eventually Pharaoh did that, and the whole nation had a comeback story.

—The Comeback, *page 9*

Reflection: A Deeper Kind of Comeback Story

Read the Overture and Chapter 1 in *The Comeback* and reflect on the following questions:

- What was a storm in your life that you thought was insurmountable? How did you see God come through and change *your* plans into *his* plans?
- What is your favorite comeback story of an underdog who, against all odds, succeeded beyond his or her dreams? What is your favorite comeback story of a champion who slipped from success but then returned to the top?

- Why do such stories give us hope? Recall times in your life when you needed hope. In what area of your life do you need a comeback right now?
- What did you learn in this session (and in the book) about the *deeper* kind of comeback that God offers? Which comeback stories from the Bible stand out to you?
- Why do comebacks begin with praising God? How does God respond to our needs when we lift our hands to him in praise?

Use the space below to write any key points or questions you want to bring to the next group meeting.

Note

1. Lawrence Kushner, *God Was in This Place, and I, I Did Not Know* (Woodstock, VT: Jewish Lights Publishing, 1991), p. 5.

SESSION **2**

PARADISE IN A
GARBAGE DUMP

No one has gone too far, and none of us has done too much, to disqualify ourselves from the love, grace, and power that Jesus can bring into our lives.

Louie Giglio

Orientation

Have you ever been out to a meal with a friend, and when the check came he or she quickly grabbed it and paid for the two of you? How do you respond to something like that? Maybe you say, "Thank you," but then quickly add, "I'll get the bill next time." Have you ever wondered why you tend to do that? Yes, it is polite, but it also exposes something about our culture: we don't know what to do with grace.

For most of us, we experience life as if there is a big scale we are trying to keep balanced. If people are generous toward us, we begin to think of ways we can "pay it back" to them. Any time our scale feels out of balance we try to even things up. It also works with negative experiences. When someone is cruel, unkind, or hurtful toward us, we are tempted to even the score. Once again our scale is out of balance, and we feel that person owes us restitution. We are going to keep things fair.

But here's the thing . . .

God's kingdom is not about scales or keeping score. It is not about keeping everything even or getting even. And it is certainly not about fairness. In God's kingdom, the reality is none of us gets what we deserve, because its economy is driven by *grace*. Grace is not fair. It does not keep score. It doesn't have a scale it's trying to balance. Instead, grace is generous, unfair, and free.

Because of this, grace is something our "pay back" culture struggles to comprehend. But, as we'll discover in this week's session, God's culture is all about the "come back." It's all about what God's grace looks like, how we access it, and what that grace means for the turnaround Jesus wants to bring in our lives.

Welcome and Checking In

Go around the group and invite everyone to answer the following questions:

- Who is the one person in your life who has helped you the most?

- What did that person do that helped you so much?

Last week, you were invited to act in the "Between-Sessions" section of the study.

- Did you do one of the activities? If so, which one?
- What are some of the things you wrote down in reflection?
- What did you learn about yourself this week?

Hearing the Word

Read aloud in the group the following passage from Luke 23:32–43. Invite everyone to listen for a fresh insight during the reading.

32 Two other men, both criminals, were also led out with him to be executed. 33 When they came to the place called the Skull, they crucified him there, along with the criminals—one on his right, the other on his left. 34 Jesus said, "Father, forgive them, for they do not know what they are doing." And they divided up his clothes by casting lots.

35 The people stood watching, and the rulers even sneered at him. They said, "He saved others; let him save himself if he is God's Messiah, the Chosen One."

36 The soldiers also came up and mocked him. They offered him wine vinegar 37 and said, "If you are the king of the Jews, save yourself."

38 There was a written notice above him, which read: THIS IS THE KING OF THE JEWS.

39 One of the criminals who hung there hurled insults at him: "Aren't you the Messiah? Save yourself and us!"

40 But the other criminal rebuked him. "Don't you fear God," he said, "since you are under the same sentence? 41 We are punished justly, for we are getting what our deeds deserve. But this man has done nothing wrong."

42 Then he said, "Jesus, remember me when you come into your kingdom."

43 Jesus answered him, "Truly I tell you, today you will be with me in paradise."

Turn to the person next to you and take turns sharing your answers to the following questions:

Have you heard this story before? If not, what stood out to you most? If you have, did you notice anything new?

Jesus forgave the people who were crucifying him. Which is harder for you: to forgive the people who hurt you or to receive forgiveness when you hurt someone else? Why?

Where do you hear "good news" in the Luke passage?

Watch the Video

Play the video segment for Session 2. As you watch, use the following outline to record any thoughts or concepts that stand out to you.

Notes
The gospel at its core isn't about being bad or being good. The Bible says it's worse than that—our sin makes us dead, and we can't do one single thing to help ourselves.

Jesus came because he is the only one who can bring us from death to everlasting life. That is the hope of the greatest comeback of all.

The lesson of the thief who asked Jesus to remember him is that if we call out to Christ for mercy, he will reach out to us with salvation.

The lesson of the other thief is that if we want the grace of God to rush into our world and bring paradise to our mess, we have to admit we need it.

The simple admission, *We need Jesus to remember us*—that humility of heart and lowering of our own estimation of ourselves—is the doorway to hearing those words from Christ.

There is nothing we have done, no decision we have made, and no distance we have traveled that is so great that if we called out to Jesus right now, he wouldn't respond to us and say, "Today, I will bring paradise into your world."

There is nothing *easy* about the grace of God that comes to us today. We receive it freely, but it cost God everything.

If Jesus said it was finished on the cross, we need to believe that is true. It doesn't matter how far we think we have gone. Even at the very end, we have the choice to either blame God or ask him for mercy today.

Group Discussion

Take a few minutes with your group members to discuss what you just watched and explore these concepts in Scripture.

First Impressions

1. Before everyone shares in the large group, turn to one or two people next to you and finish this sentence: "After watching the video, one question I now have is . . . "

Community Reflection

2. In the video, Louie said that "Jesus came not to make bad people good people but to give us everlasting life." What does this mean to you?

3. There are two thieves in the story. How would you define the difference between them? Which one do you relate to most right now?

4. Jesus wasn't drawn to those whose lives were "perfectly" put together but to those whose lives *weren't* all together. What hope does this give you in your situation?

5. There was nothing easy about Jesus forgiving the thief and saying, "Today you will be with me in paradise." Why do you think this is the case?

6. What is *mercy*? Come up with a definition as a group, and try not to use the word *grace* in your definition.

7. In the video, Louie said that "there is enough mercy in Christ for us all." Do you think this is true? Why or why not? How have you personally seen the mercy of Christ?

Opening Up to the Comeback

For this activity, you will need a table, a bucket or pitcher, water, and several small decorating stones, pebbles, or river rocks (one per participant).

This session of *The Comeback* has been about the radical and unearnable mercy of God. God offers this to everyone free of charge, yet as divinely initiated as that mercy is, there is still a part for us to play.

In Matthew 5:7, Jesus tells his listeners, "Blessed are the merciful, for they will be shown mercy." In saying this, Jesus reveals an important point about the way in which God's divine mercy flows. "Blessed are the merciful, for they will be shown mercy," is not a currency exchange formula through which we earn mercy—meaning, if we show enough mercy, we will receive some in return. Rather, it is an indication that the pathway through which God's mercy travels to us is the *same* pathway through which we pass it on to others. If we cut off the pathway to one, we automatically cut it off from the other. That, Jesus shows us, is how it works. If our heart is open to showing mercy to others, it will be open to receiving it as well.

With this in mind, for this week's "Opening Up to the Comeback," you are going to practice showing mercy. Begin by taking a stone from the pile on the table. When each person is holding one, you will consider a place in your life where someone has wronged you. The stone in your hand will represent the offense. Squeeze it while you remember what happened in order to connect the two together.

When everyone is ready, step forward and drop your stone into the bucket of water. By dropping the stone, you are letting go of your right to punish, or take revenge against, the other person. In other words, you are showing *mercy*. Now, dropping your stone does not mean that everything is okay, that all is miraculously forgiven, or that there will not be more work to do with God. All it means for this moment is that you are doing your part to keep open the path of mercy to your heart.

Closing Prayer

Once everyone is finished, follow up with a few of these questions:

- What was your reaction as you let go of the stone and dropped it in the bucket? Was it difficult for you to extend mercy? Why?
- How would your walk with God be different if you were a better mercy *giver*? How would it be different if you were a better mercy *receiver*?
- In what ways is God calling you to extend mercy to others each day? How do you feel he is calling you to receive his mercy?

Close the session by praying the Lord's Prayer together:

Our Father in heaven, hallowed be your name. Your kingdom come, your will be done, on earth as it is in heaven. Give us today our daily bread. And forgive us our sins, as we also forgive those who sin against us. And lead us not into temptation, but deliver us from the evil one. For yours is the kingdom and the power and the glory, for ever and ever. Amen. (See Matthew 6:9–13.)

BETWEEN-SESSIONS PERSONAL STUDY

Further explore the good news of *The Comeback* this week by engaging in any or all of the following between-sessions activities. *Be sure to read the reflection questions after each activity and make a few notes in your guide about the experience.* There will be a time for you to share these reflections at the beginning of the next session.

Action: Pray for Mercy

In the video this week, Louie discusses how the simple admission that *we need Jesus to remember us* is the doorway to hearing words of mercy from Christ. With this in mind, you are invited to take the practical step of going to God in prayer to seek his mercy in your life. Begin by reading the following quotes from Christian history about God's mercy:

> *God's mercy is his tenderhearted, loving compassion for his people. It is his tenderness of heart toward the needy. If grace contemplates humans as sinful, guilty, and condemned, mercy sees them as miserable and needy* (Millard Erickson).[1]

This is the first work of God—that He is merciful to all who are ready to do without their own opinion, right, wisdom, and all spiritual goods, and willing to be poor in spirit (Martin Luther).[2]

God is pleased to show mercy to his enemies, according to his own sovereign pleasure. Though he is infinitely above all, and stands in no need of creatures; yet he is graciously pleased to take a merciful notice of poor worms in the dust (Jonathan Edwards).[3]

Mercy is kindness exercised toward the miserable, and includes pity, compassion, forbearance, and gentleness, which the Scriptures so abundantly ascribe to God (Charles Hodge).[4]

Reflect on these quotes for a moment and consider which description of mercy resonates with you the most and which resonates with you the least. Once you have considered these words on mercy, it's your turn.

Think about how you would define mercy in your own words. Use the space below to write your prayer to God. After you've got something you are happy with, write the prayer on a separate sheet of paper, index card, or even a sticky note. Put it somewhere where you will see it daily, and pray it throughout the week.

Consider how the prayer affects your relationship with God, your family, and neighbors, and make some notes about it to share with the group next week.

[A great comeback] springs from simple faith from a heart that believes enough to pray a basic prayer: Jesus, please remember me. *That prayer only requires a breath, just enough to change the direction of our eternity ... We aren't blessed by God because we're better than anyone else. We get to heaven because of a simple prayer of faith.*

—The Comeback, *page 31*

Contemplation: Weak Is the New Strong

For this week's contemplation, read these words from Paul on strength in weakness from 2 Corinthians 12:5–10:

[5] *I will not boast about myself, except about my weaknesses.* [6] *Even if I should choose to boast, I would not be a fool, because I would be speaking the truth. But I refrain, so no one will think more of me than is warranted by what I do or say,* [7] *or because of these surpassingly great revelations. Therefore, in order to keep me from becoming conceited, I was given a thorn in my flesh, a messenger of Satan, to torment me.* [8] *Three times I pleaded with the Lord to take it away from me.* [9] *But he said to me, "My grace is sufficient for you, for my power is made perfect in weakness." Therefore I will boast all the more gladly about my weaknesses, so that Christ's power may rest on me.* [10] *That is why, for Christ's sake, I delight in weaknesses, in insults, in hardships, in persecutions, in difficulties. For when I am weak, then I am strong.*

Have you ever been water skiing? If you have, then you know how strange and counterintuitive it is. Water skiing does not work the way you would think. You sit in the water, skis on your feet, with the goal of getting on top of the water. Most beginners, as soon as the boat starts pulling them, try their hardest to stand up on the water.

But that won't work.

If you want to get up on your skis, you have to let the boat pull you up. If you struggle, fight, or strive, it won't happen. But if you settle back and stop trying so hard to get up, the momentum of the boat will do most of the work for you. Water skiing is counterintuitive. As it turns out, so is the kingdom of God.

In the passage from 2 Corinthians 12, Paul describes a scenario to which we can all relate. He has a "thorn in his flesh"— a problem, vice, or character flaw—that he cannot seem to shake. He has been praying that the Lord would remove it from him. Yet the word he has received back from God is, "My grace is sufficient for you, for my power is made perfect in weakness."

Such an answer flies in the face of how we think we should approach our shortcomings. Shouldn't we make an action plan, attack our flaws with everything we have, and celebrate when they fade away? The answer, apparently, is not always. There are some things in our lives in which God's glory is best revealed not in overcoming our weaknesses but in the way we surrender and receive Jesus in the midst of them.

In many ways, this is as counterintuitive as allowing the boat to pull us up on water skis. Yet it is the mysterious way the kingdom of God works in our lives.

What is the wrong way to "boast in your weakness"? What is the right way?

Where have you seen power made perfect in weakness?

What does it mean that God's grace is sufficient for us? How is that good news?

Where would you most like to see God's power be made perfect in your life this week?

A person who prays, Jesus, please remember me, *is a person who needs a comeback. The prayer is that somehow God hasn't forgotten us in this crazy world. Although we may be completely lost in despair and darkness and winter without Christmas, God holds out hope that we may come back to him . . . Or even though we've made a huge mistake that's resulted in a complete mess, there's still hope. That's the heart of a powerful prayer from a heart that desperately needs God.* God, please don't forget me. God, please remember me.

—The Comeback, *pages 28–29*

Reflection: Paradise in a Garbage Dump

Read Chapter 2 in *The Comeback* and reflect on the following questions:

- What does the story at the beginning of this chapter tell you about the way God calls people into his comeback story? How can you relate to this story?
- In Jesus' last hours on earth, God chose to put him in close proximity to two really messed-up people. Why is that important? What does this tell you about the way in which God reaches out to you with his salvation?
- How did each of the thieves react to Jesus? How is that similar to the way people react to his message today?
- In what ways did the thief who asked Jesus for mercy show he understood the gravity of his situation? In what ways have you also asked God to remember you?
- What hope does the story of this thief bring to you?

What does it tell you about the extent of God's mercy? About being "too far gone" to experience a real comeback in your life?

Use the space below to write any key points or questions you want to bring to the next group meeting.

Notes
1. Millard J. Erickson, *Christian Theology* (Grand Rapids, MI: Baker Academic, 1998), p. 322.
2. Martin Luther, cited in *What Luther Says: An Anthology* (St. Louis, MO: Concordia Publishing House, 1986), vol. 3, p. 176.
3. Jonathan Edwards, cited in *The Works of Jonathan Edwards* (Peabody, MA: Hendrickson Publishers, 1993), vol. 2, p. 110.
4. Charles Hodge, *Systematic Theology* (Phillipsburg, NJ: P&R Publishing, 1997), p. 471.

SESSION 3

WHEN DREAMS ARE DASHED

Whether we can see it or not, the same God who has called us to our dreams will steward them until they come to the conclusion God has designed. Heaven still has a plan for us.

Louie Giglio

Orientation

The last five years have introduced us to a new way of watching television. It's called *binge watching*. This occurs when you watch multiple episodes of a program in a row because "it's so good you just can't stop." What sets the hook for those who binge watch is, without a doubt, the cliffhanger ending.

Cliffhanger endings have been around for decades, and they all work the same way. The conflict and drama of the story is brought to a head, and the main characters are left in an impossible situation with no apparent way to escape. As a binge watcher, you just *have* to find out what happens next!

If you think about it, this is a bit of an odd phenomenon, because in a way we're delighting in the peril of our heroes. Not because we are sadistic, but because we know the writers have some trick up their sleeve to get our heroes out of their jam. In short, we don't fear cliffhangers because we trust we are in the hands of a master storyteller.

Our lives can feel like cliffhangers too.

Whether it is divorce, abuse, the death of a child, addiction, losing our job, or declaring bankruptcy, there are plenty of circumstances we encounter in life that feel dark. What's more, in our darkness we don't know how we will ever get out of it. We want things resolved. We want things healed. We want our pain to go away—and go away *now*.

But sometimes, we have to wait. We have to leave our cliffhanger unresolved. In these situations, when we are in the middle of it, we can find it very hard to trust God.

Here's the good news, though: we have a God who can be trusted to work our lives toward goodness and redemption no matter what we come up against. He is a God who is healing and redeeming everything for his glory. So it doesn't matter how scary the cliffhanger is, because we can always trust God to bring goodness out of it. If we hang on, we are sure to discover that we are in the hands of a Master Storyteller.

This reality is what this session is all about. What do we do when our dreams are dashed and our hope is lost? When our life is in the midst of a cliffhanger? Let's jump in and find out.

Welcome and Checking In

Go around the group and invite everyone to answer the following questions:

- This week, we will be reading about some of the literal dreams of Joseph, recorded in the book of Genesis. What is the best dream you've had that you can remember?

- What is one of the stranger dreams you've had that you can share?

Last week, you were invited to act in the "Between-Sessions" section of the study.

- Did you do one of the activities? If so, which one? If not, why not?
- What are some of the things you wrote down in reflection?
- What did you learn about yourself this week?

Hearing the Word

Read aloud in the group the following passages from Genesis 37:1–9, 18–28, and 50:15–21. Invite everyone to listen for a fresh insight during the reading.

37:1 Jacob lived in the land where his father had stayed, the land of Canaan.

2 This is the account of Jacob's family line.

Joseph, a young man of seventeen, was tending the flocks with his brothers, the sons of Bilhah and the sons of Zilpah, his father's wives, and he brought their father a bad report about them.

3 Now Israel loved Joseph more than any of his other sons, because he had been born to him in his old age; and he made an ornate robe for him. 4 When his brothers saw that their father loved him more than any of them, they hated him and could not speak a kind word to him.

5 Joseph had a dream, and when he told it to his brothers, they hated him all the more. 6 He said to them, "Listen to this dream I had: 7 We were binding sheaves of grain out in the field when suddenly my sheaf rose and stood upright, while your sheaves gathered around mine and bowed down to it."

8 His brothers said to him, "Do you intend to reign over us? Will you actually rule us?" And they hated him all the more because of his dream and what he had said.

9 Then he had another dream, and he told it to his brothers. "Listen," he said, "I had another dream, and this time the sun and moon and eleven stars were bowing down to me." . . .

18 But they saw him in the distance, and before he reached them, they plotted to kill him.

¹⁹ *"Here comes that dreamer!" they said to each other.*
²⁰ *"Come now, let's kill him and throw him into one of these cis-terns and say that a ferocious animal devoured him. Then we'll see what comes of his dreams."*

²¹ *When Reuben heard this, he tried to rescue him from their hands. "Let's not take his life," he said.* ²² *"Don't shed any blood. Throw him into this cistern here in the wilderness, but don't lay a hand on him." Reuben said this to rescue him from them and take him back to his father.*

²³ *So when Joseph came to his brothers, they stripped him of his robe—the ornate robe he was wearing—* ²⁴ *and they took him and threw him into the cistern. The cistern was empty; there was no water in it.*

²⁵ *As they sat down to eat their meal, they looked up and saw a caravan of Ishmaelites coming from Gilead. Their camels were loaded with spices, balm and myrrh, and they were on their way to take them down to Egypt.*

²⁶ *Judah said to his brothers, "What will we gain if we kill our brother and cover up his blood?* ²⁷ *Come, let's sell him to the Ishmaelites and not lay our hands on him; after all, he is our brother, our own flesh and blood." His brothers agreed.*

²⁸ *So when the Midianite merchants came by, his brothers pulled Joseph up out of the cistern and sold him for twenty shekels of silver to the Ishmaelites, who took him to Egypt . . .*

^{50:15} *When Joseph's brothers saw that their father was dead, they said, "What if Joseph holds a grudge against us and pays us back for all the wrongs we did to him?"* ¹⁶ *So they sent word to Joseph, saying, "Your father left these instructions before he died:* ¹⁷ *'This is what you are to say to Joseph: I ask you to forgive your brothers the sins and the wrongs they committed in treating you so badly.' Now please forgive*

the sins of the servants of the God of your father." When their message came to him, Joseph wept.

[18] His brothers then came and threw themselves down before him. "We are your slaves," they said.

[19] But Joseph said to them, "Don't be afraid. Am I in the place of God? [20] You intended to harm me, but God intended it for good to accomplish what is now being done, the saving of many lives. [21] So then, don't be afraid. I will provide for you and your children." And he reassured them and spoke kindly to them.

Turn to the person next to you and take turns sharing your answers to the following questions:

What is one detail that stood out to you from this story?

In the video today, we will fill in the details between what happened from the time Joseph was shipped off to Egypt and the end of the story, when he forgave his brothers. However, as you look at these two parts of the story, what do they reveal to you about Joseph?

At the end of the story, Joseph told his brothers that what they intended for harm God intended for good. How does that work in our lives today? How have you seen God take something meant for evil and leverage it for something good?

Watch the Video

Play the video segment for Session 3. As you watch, use the following outline to record any thoughts or concepts that stand out to you.

Notes

All of us at times are confronted with challenges that leave us asking, *God, what is happening to me? Where are you in the midst of this crisis?*

Regardless of what we are facing today, we have the hope that our God is working in our lives. The same God who calls us to a dream is faithful to bring that dream to fruition.

The story of Joseph in the Bible is an excellent example of how God works behind the scenes to bring the dreams he has given us to reality.

Even when Joseph went to be a servant in Potiphar's house, the Bible tells us the Lord was with him. God never abandons Joseph, even when it seems the dream has dissolved completely.

We can have confidence that even when the circumstances don't add up—when we, perhaps like Joseph, can't see God's involvement in our lives—the Lord is still always with us.

In one move, God brought Joseph from the prison to the palace. God used him to interpret a nation-shaping dream for all of Egypt and the region.

When the time is right, God can likewise take us from wherever we are to exactly where he wants us to be.

Joseph was given the opportunity to seek revenge against his brothers, but through his experiences he was able to see the long arc of the hand of God.

Our opportunity is to lean into God right now, remain faithful, and believe all over again that in spite of what we see in the present, our God isn't finished with us yet.

Group Discussion

Take a few minutes with your group members to discuss what you just watched and explore these concepts in Scripture.

First Impressions

1. Before everyone shares in the large group, turn to one or two people next to you and finish this sentence: "After watching the video, one question I now have is . . . "

Community Reflection

2. What is a dream or goal you know God has given to you?

3. Are you carrying that dream in anticipation that God will bring it to fulfillment, or do you feel as if that dream has been dashed? Explain.

4. How do you think Joseph felt when he was in prison and things seemed to be falling apart? How do you cope when things are falling apart in your life?

5. When the time is right, God can move us exactly into the position where he wants us to be. Do you find it easy or hard to trust in this truth? Why?

6. What does it look like for you to "hear" God? How does it work in your life?

7. When the chips are down, we can either blame God or trust in God. Why do you think we tend to blame God when things don't go the way we want? What does it look like to believe in God—and be grateful for his blessings—even when things don't go well?

Opening Up to the Comeback

For this activity, you will need a table, one candle per group member, and matches or a lighter.

The video this week ends with a powerful encouragement to "lean in" and believe that even when things feel hopeless and look bleak, God is still working behind the scenes. Our stories are not finished yet. In this week's "Opening Up to the Comeback," we are going to participate in an exercise to help us enter into this kind of trust.

Gather with your group members around the table you have set up and make sure each person has a candle. Close your eyes and, in silence, think of the place in your life in which you most struggle to trust that God is working. This could be a relationship with a family member, uncertainty at work, or even a health concern that does not seem to be improving. Once you've identified your area, imagine the candle is a symbol of it.

As you are ready, literally "lean in" and place the candle on the table in front of you. Once everyone's candles are on the table, take turns lighting them. Allow the lighting of the candle to be a symbol of entrusting this circumstance and struggle to God. Let it be a reminder that even when you can't see how things will turn out for good, God is still at work in your life. In short, lighting the candle is a demonstration that you want to trust God, not blame him.

Closing Prayer

After all the candles are placed and lit, take as much time as you need in silence. Close the session by praying together for a couple of minutes. In particular, pray that those in your group will experience a comeback and come to understand how God is working behind the scenes to make the dreams he has given them a reality. Pray that God will fill each person with hope and bring the encouragement they need to continue forward.

BETWEEN-SESSIONS PERSONAL STUDY

Further explore the good news of *The Comeback* this week by engaging in any or all of the following between-sessions activities. *Be sure to read the reflection questions after each activity and make a few notes in your guide about the experience.* There will be a time for you to share these reflections at the beginning of the next session.

Action: Finding God in Unexpected Places

In the video this week, Louie suggests, "It doesn't matter what we see with our eyes; God is working whether we can see it or not." To this end, you are invited to engage in an exercise that will help you be more aware of the workings and presence of God around you.

Grab a pen and a notepad and go to a public place you visit often. This could be the public library, a shopping mall, a coffee shop, a city park, or elsewhere. Find a place to sit where you can journal, and take in what's happening around you. Then pray, *God, show me where you are already on display in this place and in these people.* As you pray, pay attention to what you observe. Where do you see God in places you did not expect?

For anyone who is feeling adventurous, do this same exercise in a place outside your comfort zone. This could be a hospital, a neighborhood with people who are different from you, or even a location in town where the homeless congregate. See what happens when you pray this prayer in those places.

The more you seek God in the unexpected and uncomfortable places of your daily life, the more you will train yourself to find him working in your struggles and difficulties.

Go. Pray. God is near.

Make a few notes about your experience to share with the group next week.

Through the lens of God's grace, we can look back on the thirteen lost years of Joseph's life and see that these were actually saving years, not only for Joseph, but for his entire family and many others. If we can grasp that one idea, it frees us from feeling we are in charge of any circumstances. We are released to trust our lives into the hands of a loving God.

—The Comeback, *page 50*

Contemplation: Bringing Good Work to Completion

For this week's contemplation, read these words from Paul in Philippians 1:3–11 on the work God is doing in each of us:

> ³ *I thank my God every time I remember you.* ⁴ *In all my prayers for all of you, I always pray with joy* ⁵ *because of your partnership in the gospel from the first day until now,* ⁶ *being confident of this, that he who began a good work in you will carry it on to completion until the day of Christ Jesus.*
>
> ⁷ *It is right for me to feel this way about all of you, since I have you in my heart and, whether I am in chains or defending and confirming the gospel, all of you share in God's grace with me.* ⁸ *God can testify how I long for all of you with the affection of Christ Jesus.*
>
> ⁹ *And this is my prayer: that your love may abound more and more in knowledge and depth of insight,* ¹⁰ *so that you may be able to discern what is best and may be pure and blameless for the day of Christ,* ¹¹ *filled with the fruit of righteousness that comes through Jesus Christ—to the glory and praise of God.*

During tough times in our lives, we often become discontent, frustrated, and disappointed—and desperately want to resolve the tension we are facing. We call out to God, "Help me! Please fix this!" The irony, however, is that sometimes God himself allows these experiences.

In the passage above, Paul speaks of God beginning a good work in us (see verse 6). This is something we trust as Christians. We believe God is moving in our lives and working out the rhythms of salvation one day at a time. One item we tend to overlook, however, is that the good work God is doing sometimes involves *disrupting our status quo*.

For instance, we may have habits and attitudes that are *not* part of God's good plan for us. So the day comes when the "good work" God is doing involves changing those habits and attitudes. When this happens we may feel stuck, stagnant, and frustrated, because something that used to help us get by is not working anymore. We then ask God for help, but the truth is he is already helping us. He disrupted our lives to bring to an end the destructive patterns, habits, and ideologies and to give us something much better.

This is why the second half of verse 6 is so hopeful. Just as God has begun a good work in us, he "will carry it on to completion until the day of Christ Jesus." If God started a work within us, we can rest assured that he will be faithful to finish it. So we should take heart: even when we cannot see God, he is there, bringing everything to fulfillment in our lives and in the world.

What do you feel is the "good work" God has been doing in you recently?

Have you ever had a season of "divine frustration" as the above devotional describes? What was it?

Is there anything you've been working on with God that you are eager for him to "bring to completion"? Explain.

What three words would you use to craft a prayer to God about this area? Write them below, and pray about them this week.

Chances are good that you once had a dream—a big, noble, beautiful dream—that you could envision coming true, but that dream was snatched away. An experience like that leaves you longing for a comeback . . . If you're going through something similar right now, know that God still has a plan to use your life in a significant way. That thought may be just a seed in your heart for now, but it can grow into a great truth . . . Jesus is a dream restorer. Your dream might look different now than when it was born in your heart, but heaven still has a plan for you.

—The Comeback, *page 40*

Reflection: When Dreams Are Dashed

Read Chapter 3 in *The Comeback* and reflect on the following questions:

- In the opening story of Jarryd Wallace, how were his dreams of running—perhaps in the Olympics—dashed? How did he respond? How did God ultimately use the situation to bring about an even greater dream?
- What is a dream you've had that seems to have been snatched away? What type of comeback do you need today to restore your hope in God's faithfulness to bring about that dream—or an even greater one?
- Joseph went from dreamer to slave to prisoner. How can you relate to his story? In what areas of life do you feel like you are in a prison?
- What do you think enabled Joseph to never lose sight of the fact that God was working in his story? How did his circumstances train him and shape him for the work God wanted him to do?
- How can you, like Joseph, see your story as part of God's story? Know that God is going the distance with you? See your experience as a salvation story?

Use the space below to write any key points or questions you want to bring to the next group meeting.

SESSION 4

NEVER TOO LATE

*We have not gone too far for God to intervene
and use our life again. No one has done too much
that God can't step into the story.*

Louie Giglio

Orientation

For most people, hair spray is just something to keep their hair in place after they have styled it. Nothing more, nothing less. However, for the more devious among us, we know there are other uses for hair spray as well.

Before modern safety standards were put in place, a can of hair spray was highly combustible. Manufacturers placed warnings on the label about not using the product near an open flame or while smoking. Of course, if you chose to ignore these warnings and sprayed the can at an open flame, it made a pretty nice blowtorch—to the great delight of anyone watching. (Not that *you* would know anything about that, right?)

Many of our most basic desires are things over which we have no control. At least, not in their initial stages. Someone hurts us, and we are instantly overwhelmed with a desire for revenge. We see another person who fits our definition of attractive, and we feel a wave of desire. We come into extra money and we have an impulse to hoard it and spend it selfishly.

When these desires come over us, it's as if a fire is lit within us, and that little flame just sits there and flickers. At this point we have a choice: we can let it burn out, or we hit it with a burst of hair spray.

That moment of decision is what this session of *The Comeback* is all about. It is about the temptation we feel to nurture and fuel the sin in our lives so it burns hot—yet also potentially burns us out. If you recognize this dynamic in your life or feel like something you used to play with has now got its hooks in you, this session is for you!

Welcome and Checking In

Go around the group and ask everyone to finish this statement:

"When it comes to food, my one weakness is _____
_____."

Last week, you were invited to act in the "Between-Sessions" section of the study.

- Did you do one of the activities? If so, which one? If not, why not?
- What are some of the things you wrote down in reflection?
- What did you learn about yourself this week?
- What did you learn about God this week?

Hearing the Word

Read aloud in the group the following passage from Judges 16:1–22. Invite everyone to listen for a fresh insight during the reading.

> *¹ One day Samson went to Gaza, where he saw a prostitute. He went in to spend the night with her. ² The people of Gaza were told, "Samson is here!" So they surrounded the place and lay in wait for him all night at the city gate. They made no move during the night, saying, "At dawn we'll kill him."*
>
> *³ But Samson lay there only until the middle of the night. Then he got up and took hold of the doors of the city gate, together with*

the two posts, and tore them loose, bar and all. He lifted them to his shoulders and carried them to the top of the hill that faces Hebron.

⁴ Some time later, he fell in love with a woman in the Valley of Sorek whose name was Delilah. ⁵ The rulers of the Philistines went to her and said, "See if you can lure him into showing you the secret of his great strength and how we can overpower him so we may tie him up and subdue him. Each one of us will give you eleven hundred shekels of silver."

⁶ So Delilah said to Samson, "Tell me the secret of your great strength and how you can be tied up and subdued."

⁷ Samson answered her, "If anyone ties me with seven fresh bowstrings that have not been dried, I'll become as weak as any other man."

⁸ Then the rulers of the Philistines brought her seven fresh bowstrings that had not been dried, and she tied him with them. ⁹ With men hidden in the room, she called to him, "Samson, the Philistines are upon you!" But he snapped the bowstrings as easily as a piece of string snaps when it comes close to a flame. So the secret of his strength was not discovered.

¹⁰ Then Delilah said to Samson, "You have made a fool of me; you lied to me. Come now, tell me how you can be tied."

¹¹ He said, "If anyone ties me securely with new ropes that have never been used, I'll become as weak as any other man."

¹² So Delilah took new ropes and tied him with them. Then, with men hidden in the room, she called to him, "Samson, the Philistines are upon you!" But he snapped the ropes off his arms as if they were threads.

¹³ Delilah then said to Samson, "All this time you have been making a fool of me and lying to me. Tell me how you can be tied."

He replied, "If you weave the seven braids of my head into the fabric on the loom and tighten it with the pin, I'll become as weak

*as any other man." So while he was sleeping, Delilah took the seven
braids of his head, wove them into the fabric* ¹⁴ *and tightened it with
the pin.*

*Again she called to him, "Samson, the Philistines are upon
you!" He awoke from his sleep and pulled up the pin and the loom,
with the fabric.*

¹⁵ *Then she said to him, "How can you say, 'I love you,' when
you won't confide in me? This is the third time you have made a fool
of me and haven't told me the secret of your great strength."* ¹⁶ *With
such nagging she prodded him day after day until he was sick to
death of it.*

¹⁷ *So he told her everything. "No razor has ever been used on
my head," he said, "because I have been a Nazirite dedicated to
God from my mother's womb. If my head were shaved, my strength
would leave me, and I would become as weak as any other man."*

¹⁸ *When Delilah saw that he had told her everything, she sent
word to the rulers of the Philistines, "Come back once more; he has
told me everything." So the rulers of the Philistines returned with
the silver in their hands.* ¹⁹ *After putting him to sleep on her lap, she
called for someone to shave off the seven braids of his hair, and so
began to subdue him. And his strength left him.*

²⁰ *Then she called, "Samson, the Philistines are upon you!"*

*He awoke from his sleep and thought, "I'll go out as before and
shake myself free." But he did not know that the LORD had left him.*

²¹ *Then the Philistines seized him, gouged out his eyes and took
him down to Gaza. Binding him with bronze shackles, they set him
to grinding grain in the prison.* ²² *But the hair on his head began to
grow again after it had been shaved.*

Turn to the person next to you and take turns sharing your
answers to the following questions:

What stood out to you when you heard this story read? What new detail did you notice that you hadn't recognized before?

What does this small portion of Samson's story reveal about his character?

What temptations was Samson facing in this story? How did he respond? What was the result of his actions?

Watch the Video

Play the video segment for Session 4. As you watch, use the following outline to record any thoughts or concepts that stand out to you.

Notes

The nature of temptation is that it works little by little. Day by day, we take little steps that build a path, build a habit, build a highway, that leads us to a place we never intended to be.

We have to be honest about the "river" that is flowing within us. Is it a river of life leading to abundance? Or is it a river of deception that will ultimately steal life from us?

Sometimes we need a comeback not because of any outside circumstances that happened to us, but because we made conscious decisions that landed us in our current state.

Samson was a leader of God's people—a judge with great strength because of God's power on him. He was a major warrior for God, but inwardly he had a great weakness for women.

The name *Delilah* means "low-hanging fruit." This is what the enemy does—places low-hanging fruit in our weakness that leads us to total collapse.

God gave Samson a comeback story at the end of his life in spite of all the mistakes he had made. His story shows us again that we can never do too much or stray too far that God can't step into the story and allow his Spirit to come back to us.

Samson's story also shows that if we're on a path to destruction, *now* is the time to jump off that path and ask God for a new start.

This requires us to be *transparent* and *vulnerable*. It takes us saying to the people around us, "I may look strong, but I am weak. You may see the good in me, but there is something I'm harboring in my heart that will be the end of me if I don't bring it to light."

Group Discussion

Take a few minutes with your group members to discuss what you just watched and explore these concepts in Scripture.

First Impressions

1. Before everyone shares in the large group, turn to one or two people next to you and finish this sentence: "After watching the video, one question I now have is . . . "

Community Reflection

2. In what ways does the enemy use temptation to take us farther and farther down the wrong path? Why is this such an effective tactic?

3. Delilah represented "low-hanging fruit" in Samson's life—a temptation the enemy put right at eye level. In what ways have you found this to be a typical pattern of the enemy? Where have you seen it?

4. Is it easy or difficult for you to be vulnerable with others? Why?

5. What are some of the struggles you face when it comes to being transparent and open about your weaknesses?

6. Who is one person in your life you can be totally honest with?

7. What do you think it looks like, in flesh and blood, to "receive God's path and walk on it"?

Opening Up to the Comeback

For this activity, each participant will need a blank piece of paper and a pen.

In this session, we saw that if we are on a path to destruction, *now* is the time to jump off that path and ask God for a comeback. The way in which we do this is twofold.

First, we must be *transparent* and *vulnerable*. When we tell the truth about our weaknesses in front of one another and in front of God, those things start to lose their power. God begins healing, and restoration occurs. Second, we have to be *open* to the new path that God has for us—the path that leads to life and abundance instead of destruction.

This week, you are going to get the chance to respond to this invitation. Take a piece of paper and a pen, and then spend five to ten minutes apart from the others in the group. During that time, write down on the paper the place in your life where you experience the most temptation. In other words, what is the "river of destruction" running through your heart? Then turn the paper over and write down the name of the person with whom you are going to share this struggle during the week.

When the group gathers back together, invite people to reflect on the activity by discussing the following questions:

- Was it hard or easy to know what to write on your paper?
- Does the thought of sharing what's on your paper make you feel heavier or lighter? Why?
- Why do you feel it is important to deal with this particular struggle? Where do you feel it is leading you?

Closing Prayer

Close the session by praying the Lord's Prayer with each other. Pay special attention to the portions about temptation and forgiveness.

Our Father in heaven, hallowed be your name. Your kingdom come, your will be done, on earth as it is in heaven. Give us today our daily bread. And forgive us our sins, as we also forgive those who sin against us. And lead us not into temptation, but deliver us from the evil one. For yours is the kingdom and the power and the glory, for ever and ever. Amen. (See Matthew 6:9–13.)

BETWEEN-SESSIONS PERSONAL STUDY

Further explore the good news of *The Comeback* this week by engaging in any or all of the following between-sessions activities. *Be sure to read the reflection questions after each activity and make a few notes in your guide about the experience.* There will be a time for you to share these reflections at the beginning of the next session.

Action: Confession

During this week's "Opening Up to the Comeback," you were invited to start on a journey of transparency, vulnerability, and new choices. You took time to pray and write down your greatest area of temptation and one person with whom you could share it. The concept behind this process is that by sharing your weakness with someone else, it robs it of its power. Once your darkness is in the light, the shame and claim it has over you dissipates.

This kind of vulnerability will open you up to God's love and power in fresh ways. With an accountability partner in the mix, you have someone to help you chart new paths where you need them. You have an encourager who can remind you of God's love and forgiveness for you no matter what you've done.

Your *Action* this week is simply to follow through on this plan and share your struggles with someone—to jump off any paths leading to destruction and step onto God's path of life. Remember, in so doing you are following a simple admonition from the book of James: "Therefore confess your sins to each other and pray for each other so that you may be healed. The prayer of a righteous person is powerful and effective" (5:16). Also, don't forget to discuss with the person you have chosen what *specific steps* you will take to train yourself in new habits.

After you have done this, take time to reflect on the experience: What was it like for you? What did you learn about yourself? Was it helpful? Why or why not? Will you go back and see the person with whom you shared your weakness? Why or why not?

Make a few notes about your experience to share with the group next week.

Maybe you're in some really difficult place because of an act of foolishness. You can choose to curse the place you're in, or you can remember that it's your fault you're there. The way out is to admit, "It was me who got myself here," and you can take a direct route through the grace of Jesus back to God. By repentance you can get back on track faster . . . Will you let [God] deliver you?

—The Comeback, page 79

Contemplation: A Way Out!

For this week's contemplation, read Paul's words about temptation in 1 Corinthians 10:12–15:

> [12] So, if you think you are standing firm, be careful that you don't fall! [13] No temptation has overtaken you except what is common to mankind. And God is faithful; he will not let you be tempted beyond what you can bear. But when you are tempted, he will also provide a way out so that you can endure it. [14] Therefore, my dear friends, flee from idolatry. [15] I speak to sensible people; judge for yourselves what I say.

Everyone has experienced temptation. It is one of the most constant and consistent parts of the human experience. There will be seasons of life when we feel as if things are going well, and we will not be afflicted by temptation. Then there will be seasons when it's all we can do to stay on track. Sometimes we can point to a reason for our temptations, while sometimes we can't. The only thing we can say for sure is that temptation leads to pain.

As if this is not difficult enough on its own, we will sometimes be barraged by a nagging little voice that creeps into our head. Call it the crazy roommate that lives in our mind, or the "little devil" on our shoulder, but the voice is always the same. It says, *No one else has this problem. Only you are struggling with it.*

This voice takes our struggles and makes them heavier to bear, as now they are draped with a cloak of shame. This shame, in turn, makes us want to be secretive about our weakness. When that happens, we find ourselves stuck in temptation instead of seeking to become free.

If you recognize this dynamic in your life, you can take away a few important principles from the 1 Corinthians 10 passage. First, Paul reminds you there is no temptation you can face that someone else hasn't stared down before. You are not alone in your struggles. You are in the same boat as everybody else. Therefore, that voice in your head—the one that says you are alone in your weakness—is a lie. Plain and simple.

Second, Paul states when it comes to the things that allure you most, God will not allow you to be tempted "beyond what you can bear" (verse 13). This claim is mysterious, because it shows that God is somehow setting boundaries on your temptations to make sure you can handle them. So why doesn't God just take away temptation and make life easier for you? Because even Jesus was led by the Holy Spirit into the wilderness to be tempted. Like Jesus, you *will* be tempted at times. But with God's help, you can overcome that temptation as Jesus did.

Third, even in your darkest moments, you have the promise that God will always give you a way out. It may not feel good to choose God's way—and it may not be easy—but you will always have access to a lifeline. So, look for it. When the chips are down and you are struggling, a helpful prayer can be, "God, show me the way out of here." This is a prayer Jesus will answer. Every time.

Notice that all this talk about temptation ends with Paul admonishing the community in Corinth not to worship idols. How are those two points connected? Well, put simply, an idol is anything we trust that is not God. The things that tempt us and cause us to struggle are usually the things on which we lean that are not God. If we trust them, even seemingly good things (like our own willpower, for example), we are sunk.

God invites us to trust him above all else, no matter what. This is hard when we are tempted, but we are not in it alone. There is always a way out. The question is, will we take it?

Do you ever hear the voice that says, "No one else has this problem; it's just you"? Explain.

Recall a time that God showed you a way out of temptation. How did you respond?

What types of things do you tend to trust instead of God? How will you change that?

In Samson's last gasp, God's power came back to him. The deliverance of all Israel started the day of Samson's swansong comeback. What he had not done in his lifetime, he did in his death, because our God is the God of the comeback. That's the lesson for us ... God is always good, and he always remembers us. Our prayer isn't to get revenge on a group of people, but it's to be strengthened once more so we might live for God's glory. We push with all our might on whatever stone pillars are keeping us bound. With God's strength renewed in us, the walls of our prisons come toppling down.

—The Comeback, *page 92*

Reflection: Never Too Late

Read Chapter 5 in *The Comeback* and reflect on the following questions:

- What was happening in Israel at the time God raised up Samson to be a judge? Why did God at times allow his people to become subject to the nations around them? What did this achieve?
- What are some of the background details the author of Judges tells us about Samson's birth? Why are those details important?
- What got in the way of Samson fulfilling all of the things God had in store for him and the Israelites? How did Samson gradually allow his temptation to take him down and out?
- How did Samson miss out on the internal exercise of God's power? How did he hold out in his sin instead of get out of it? Where did it lead him?

- Samson could have ended up a laughingstock, but because he turned back to the Lord, he ended as a champion. What was his smashing comeback? What does his story reveal about God's mercy and grace in spite of our faults?

Use the space below to write any key points or questions you want to bring to the next group meeting.

SESSION 5

GET UP

We want the miracle. We want the power. We want God to do what only God can do. But we often don't understand we have a role to play in the unfolding comeback that God wants to bring to our lives.

Louie Giglio

Orientation

During the last decade, a sport called Mixed Martial Arts has gained immense popularity in our culture. Nowhere is this more clearly demonstrated than by the addition of the phrase "tap out" to our vocabulary.

The phrase comes from the climax of an MMA contest when one fighter has the other in a hold, and the pain becomes so great the embattled athlete has to tap the mat twice to signal the referee that he is giving up. The referee then calls off the fight, and the other fighter is declared the winner. A fighter only "taps out" when he's got no fight left. When he taps out, he is giving up.

Do you know that place? The place of the tap out? When you're worn out, beat up, and tired of fighting, the idea of quitting can be an enticing prospect. Or maybe you tapped out years ago, and now you're just going through the motions. There's no passion, no zeal, no purpose left in you. You're just biding your time until it's time to check out.

But what if Jesus could intervene and bring a comeback even in the places where you have tapped out? What if Jesus wanted to intersect your story before you get to the end and give you life to the full on this side of eternity? Does that sound like good news to you?

If so, be encouraged, because this week we are going to discuss how Jesus *can* rescue you from the places where you've tapped out. He does it all the time. In fact, it's what he does best.

During this session, we will explore how it all works. So hang in there for just a few more minutes. There's a comeback brewing.

Welcome and Checking In

Go around the group and ask everyone to complete the following sentence:

"The best thing about my life right now is _____
_____."

Last week, you were invited to act in the "Between-Sessions" section of the study.

- Did you get to share your struggles with anyone? If so, how did it go? If not why not?
- Did you participate in the *Contemplation* or *Reflection* activities?
- What did you write down in reflection?
- Did you learn anything about yourself this week? Did you learn anything about God?

Hearing the Word

Read aloud in the group the following passage from Luke 7:11–17. Invite everyone to listen for a fresh insight during the reading.

[11] Soon afterward, Jesus went to a town called Nain, and his disciples and a large crowd went along with him. [12] As he approached the town gate, a dead person was being carried out—the only son of his mother, and she was a widow. And a large crowd from the town was with her. [13] When the Lord saw her, his heart went out to her and he said, "Don't cry."

¹⁴ Then he went up and touched the bier they were carrying him on, and the bearers stood still. He said, "Young man, I say to you, get up!" ¹⁵ The dead man sat up and began to talk, and Jesus gave him back to his mother.

¹⁶ They were all filled with awe and praised God. "A great prophet has appeared among us," they said. "God has come to help his people." ¹⁷ This news about Jesus spread throughout Judea and the surrounding country.

Turn to the person next to you and take turns sharing your answers to the following questions:

What was one thing that stood out to you from the story?

What are some important points that you can take away from this story?

Watch the Video

Play the video segment for Session 5. As you watch, use the following outline to record any thoughts or concepts that stand out to you.

Notes

The question for us is, what are the things in our lives that are literally carrying us out to death?

Our adversary's plan is not just to trip us up in this life but to bury us in a hole in the ground. That is why Jesus said, "The thief comes only to steal and kill and destroy" (John 10:10).

Jesus can speak life into those moments. He can snatch us out of the jaws of death and destruction and bring us back into the land of the living.

In the story of the widow of Nain told in Luke 7, Jesus instructed the woman who had lost her son not to cry. He could say this because he already knew in his heart that he was going to turn that woman's story around that day.

In Jesus' day, a religious leader would never go near a dead body. But Jesus broke through all the norms, stopped the funeral, reached onto the stretcher of death, and told the dead boy to get up. And immediately, the young man sat up and began to talk.

When we read this story, we have to wonder how much time was left before this funeral procession was the right distance out of town and this boy was buried in a hole in the ground. Likewise, how far will *we* be from the grave when Christ rescues us?

We want the miracle—for God to do only what he can do to save us—but we have a role to play in our comeback. That role is to get up out of whatever we have deceived ourselves into believing, stand on the person of Jesus, cling to him, lean toward him, and walk in the truth he is providing in our lives.

The outcome of our saying goodbye to the stretcher and yes to the One who can bring us back to life is that the story of Jesus will be told to the world.

Group Discussion

Take a few minutes with your group members to discuss what you just watched and explore these concepts in Scripture.

First Impressions
1. Before everyone shares in the large group, turn to one or two people next to you and finish this sentence: "After watching the video, one question I now have is . . . "

Community Reflection
2. What did you think about Rachel's story? Where is the "good news" in it?

3. Jesus said, "I have come that they may have life, and have it to the full" (John 10:10). How do we tend to interpret this verse? What do Jesus' words mean to you personally?

4. What kinds of things in this world lead people to their own graves?

5. What does the story of the widow of Nain reveal about the enemy's plans for us? About Jesus' plans for us?

6. How can you see yourself in this story? How has Jesus rescued you from certain death? What is he doing right now to lead you away from the path of destruction?

7. The gospel is not only about a decision you make once and for all, but it's also about a decision you make every day. How would you define "the gospel"? What do you think it means to make "gospel" decisions every day?

Opening Up to the Comeback

For this activity, each group will need a compass.

This week's session in *The Comeback* asks us a profound question: "Do we believe that things can really change?" Does tomorrow have to be the same as today, or is it possible for Jesus to intersect our lives, even on a stretcher, and do something new?

Yes! Things *can* be different. At the heart of that witness is the practice of baptism, because in baptism we get a powerful expression of a new life. When we are baptized, we go down into the water, which symbolizes the death of our former, sinful self. But then we are brought forth out of the water into the new life God has for us! We are a *new creation* in Christ. Jesus *can* make things different, and it can start today.

In the earliest expressions of the church, before people went into the water, they would stand and face the west. Why west, and not north, south, or east? Because the sun sets in the west, and so the ancient Christians used that, symbolically, to denote the darkness. The west was where the light went out.

Therefore, as a physical affirmation that they were leaving behind the works of darkness and putting on Christ's light, just before their baptism, Christians would spit toward the west! This visceral symbol of disgust, aversion, and rejection was applied to the destructive patterns and attitudes of the old life. Now that these believers were Jesus followers, they wanted to leave those things behind.

For our "Opening Up to the Comeback" this week, we are going to take a page out of these early Christians' book (without the spitting part). In the video this week, Louie emphasized that receiving new life from Jesus requires our participation. If God brings a comeback into our lives, we have a responsibility to keep that going. So today, with your group, you are going to go outside (weather permitting) and use the compass to find west. Once you have determined where west is, everyone in the group will stand and face that direction.

Next, you need to consider what destructive and unhealthy habits are getting in the way of the full life Jesus wants you to have. When you have that in mind, turn toward the east and put your back to the west. (Each person in the group should do this.) By doing so, each person will be saying, "I'm leaving behind these patterns that bring darkness into my life, and I'm facing the direction where the light breaks new each morning."

Closing Prayer

When you finish, join hands and pray together for a couple of minutes. Thank God for saving you from the stretcher and for rescuing you from the grave. Pray for those who may be moments away from destruction and that God will use your group as a witness to his power and love. Ask God to continue to give your group members a comeback.

BETWEEN-SESSIONS PERSONAL STUDY

Further explore the good news of *The Comeback* this week by engaging in any or all of the following between-sessions activities. *Be sure to read the reflection questions after each activity and make a few notes in your guide about the experience.* There will be a time for you to share these reflections at the beginning of the next session.

Action: Just Do it!

One of the hardest parts of leaving unhealthy patterns behind is just getting started. Newton's first law of motion—"an object at rest stays at rest"—can apply easily to our hearts. To be fair, of course, when we're caught up in brokenness, addiction, or pain, we are not at rest in any real sense. Nevertheless, we can create coping mechanisms we *think* are working for us, and then convince ourselves we are fine.

That's not good enough for God. God wants freedom for us. Yet we have to work with him to get the ball rolling. This exercise is all about that process.

Think of something you have been putting off doing. It might be an unwritten thank-you note, an oft-delayed project on the house, papers that need to be filed, or a phone call that needs to be returned. Whatever you choose, take one day this week and just do it! Push against the inertia that compels you to keep putting it off, and act. And when you act, act as a prayer.

When you fulfill this task, own it as a moment of training. Experience it as a place where you are rehearsing the rhythm of change in your life, so that when the hard things need to be changed, you already know the movement. Be sure to take some time to journal about what you chose to do, what it was like to finish the to-do, and then where God was in the process.

Pray. God is near.

Make a few notes about your experience to share with the group next week.

Think of it this way: we need God's saving grace to be made alive. And we need God's transforming grace to be made alive every day. The grace is the same grace. The gospel is the same gospel. We need grace to get off the stretcher for the first time. We need grace to stay off the stretcher if it ever beckons to us. And we need grace to get off the stretcher again if we succumb to the temptation of going back to our old (dead) ways.

—The Comeback, *page 138*

Contemplation:
Hearing God's Voice

For this week's contemplation, read John 10:1–10:

> *[Jesus said,] [1]"Very truly I tell you Pharisees, anyone who does not enter the sheep pen by the gate, but climbs in by some other way, is a thief and a robber. [2] The one who enters by the gate is the shepherd of the sheep. [3] The gatekeeper opens the gate for him, and the sheep listen to his voice. He calls his own sheep by name and leads them out. [4] When he has brought out all his own, he goes on ahead of them, and his sheep follow him because they know his voice. [5] But they will never follow a stranger; in fact, they will run away from him because they do not recognize a stranger's voice." [6] Jesus used this figure of speech, but the Pharisees did not understand what he was telling them.*
>
> *[7] Therefore Jesus said again, "Very truly I tell you, I am the gate for the sheep. [8] All who have come before me are thieves and robbers, but the sheep have not listened to them. [9] I am the gate; whoever enters through me will be saved. They will come in and go out, and find pasture. [10] The thief comes only to steal and kill and destroy; I have come that they may have life, and have it to the full."*

In the movies, the voice of God is often given a resonant, loud, regal-sounding tone, but what does God actually sound like? This notion of "hearing God's voice" is a theological concept that raises all kinds of compelling questions. One of these is, "If God is speaking, why is it so hard to hear him sometimes?" Questions like this can produce anxiety in us and make us wonder if we are doing something wrong. We might even conclude we don't hear from God because we're "not worthy." Do you know this anxiety?

In the video this week, we discussed Jesus' words in verse 10 and how he promised that he came to give us life and life to the full. Yet, it seems, the thief can compromise the kind of full life Jesus has for us. The thief wants to tear us down and knock us both off balance and off track. Enter Jesus as the Good Shepherd. Shepherds guide their sheep and lead the way even when the going gets tough. Shepherds know the way home; following them is simply a matter of listening for their voice.

Yet this seems to circle us right back to that earlier place of anxiety. "But I struggle to hear the Shepherd's voice," we say. "What if I'm not *spiritual enough* to hear his voice? What if I've done too much, or gone too far, to hear the Shepherd's voice?" If you've ever asked such a question, take heart, because the answer couldn't be simpler.

The sheep, Jesus says, follow him because they know his voice. That's it. They *already* know it. That means the voice of the Shepherd is not something elusive, foreign, or reserved for the elite. It's something we *already* know. We're *already* familiar with the voice of the Shepherd because we are one of his sheep. It's in us now!

So stop working so hard to hear God's voice, and just *listen*. God's way is already being laid out before you. The Shepherd is calling. Just breathe, listen, and follow.

What does it look like for you to "hear God" in your devotional life?

Do you ever have anxiety about listening for God's voice? If so, why?

What would "life to the full" look like for you this week?

What are two ways you can relax and listen for the Shepherd's voice right now?

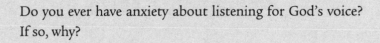

When you climb off of your stretcher, don't make the mistake of thinking that your resurrection story concludes with you. It doesn't. There's more at stake than what happens in your life. What's at stake is how God wants to raise up hope in a community, a nation, and the world to the point where people look around and see what God is doing in people's lives.

—The Comeback, *page 140*

Reflection: Get Up

Read Chapter 8 in *The Comeback* and reflect on the following questions:

- In Jesus' time, the word *stretcher* was synonymous with *coffin*. For us, the stretcher can be symbolic of the thing in our lives that is carrying us toward death. Think about what this might represent in your situation. How has the enemy used that thing to try to carry you away from the purposes of God?
- How would you define "spiritual death"? How does the story of the widow of Nain told in Luke 7:11–17 show that Jesus is Lord over both physical and spiritual death?
- How did Jesus show his authority over death in this story? How has he demonstrated that same authority in your life?
- Being dead is a big problem. If you're a corpse, you can't do anything to help yourself. And the Bible tells us that we are *all* spiritually dead. But what's the good news of the gospel? What power do we have available to us when we're tempted to lie down on our "stretchers" again?
- How did the crowd in Nain respond to witnessing this miracle? What does that tell us about the impact our lives have on others when it comes to receiving a comeback from God?

Use the space below to write any key points or questions you want to bring to the next group meeting.

SESSION **6**

JESUS IS ENOUGH

*There is a moment we discover that, no matter how
our stories turn out, Jesus is enough.*

Louie Giglio

Orientation

Do you know someone who has overcome an addiction? Most likely, their story involves a time and place when they "hit rock bottom." Meaning, they were at their lowest, darkest place in life, and in that darkness they realized they had one stark choice: change or die. Hitting rock bottom involves a great deal of pain, but it can also provide the motivation a person needs to bring about a change. But hitting rock bottom doesn't have to be the end of the story. It can actually be the beginning.

Think about the people you know who are the most steady, secure, and at peace. You may know them from church, work, school, or your family. Often they have something in common: they have endured something tragic. Maybe it was the loss of a loved one. Maybe it was a chronic disease. Maybe, due to a series of bad or unethical choices, they lost their career. Whatever it was, their serenity today comes partly from the fact that when their trauma hit, they did not shirk away, ignore, or try to numb the pain it caused. Instead, they went *through* it. Going through it is part of what, mysteriously, sets us free.

Our final session of *The Comeback* is all about the places where we have hit rock bottom. It is about the places where we have endured so much pain that we're not sure what to do next. It is about the places where we have failed. Even more, it is about the places where an earthly comeback might not be possible. Yet it is also about that mysterious thing that happens in this place of emptiness, grief, and failure: *we discover that we are not alone.* Jesus is with us!

Jesus does not wait for us to get out of our pain before we find him. Instead, he meets us *in* our pain and *transforms* it. Jesus enters our brokenness and depravity and walks us *through* to the other side so we are set free. He is the way, and his path leads to life. Yet we must have the courage to follow him!

So this week, be open and take heart. Even when you're at your lowest and no earthly comeback is possible, Jesus will meet you there. And Jesus, as it turns out, is enough.

Welcome and Checking In

Go around the group and ask everyone to complete the following sentence:

> When I hear the statement "Jesus is enough," to me it means: _____

Last week, you were invited to act in the "Between-Sessions" section of the study.

- Did you do one of the activities? If so, which one? If not, why not?
- What are some of the things you wrote down in reflection?
- What did you learn about yourself this week?

Hearing the Word

Read aloud in the group the following passage from 1 Kings 17:1–24. Invite everyone to listen for a fresh insight during the reading.

¹ Now Elijah the Tishbite, from Tishbe in Gilead, said to Ahab, "As the LORD, the God of Israel, lives, whom I serve, there will be neither dew nor rain in the next few years except at my word."

² Then the word of the LORD came to Elijah: ³ "Leave here, turn eastward and hide in the Kerith Ravine, east of the Jordan. ⁴ You will drink from the brook, and I have directed the ravens to supply you with food there."

⁵ So he did what the LORD had told him. He went to the Kerith Ravine, east of the Jordan, and stayed there. ⁶ The ravens brought him bread and meat in the morning and bread and meat in the evening, and he drank from the brook.

⁷ Some time later the brook dried up because there had been no rain in the land. ⁸ Then the word of the LORD came to him: ⁹ "Go at once to Zarephath in the region of Sidon and stay there. I have directed a widow there to supply you with food." ¹⁰ So he went to Zarephath. When he came to the town gate, a widow was there gathering sticks. He called to her and asked, "Would you bring me a little water in a jar so I may have a drink?" ¹¹ As she was going to get it, he called, "And bring me, please, a piece of bread."

¹² "As surely as the LORD your God lives," she replied, "I don't have any bread—only a handful of flour in a jar and a little olive oil in a jug. I am gathering a few sticks to take home and make a meal for myself and my son, that we may eat it—and die."

¹³ Elijah said to her, "Don't be afraid. Go home and do as you have said. But first make a small loaf of bread for me from what you have and bring it to me, and then make something for yourself and your son. ¹⁴ For this is what the LORD, the God of Israel, says: 'The jar of flour will not be used up and the jug of oil will not run dry until the day the LORD sends rain on the land.'"

¹⁵ She went away and did as Elijah had told her. So there was food every day for Elijah and for the woman and her family. ¹⁶ For

the jar of flour was not used up and the jug of oil did not run dry, in keeping with the word of the LORD spoken by Elijah.

17 Some time later the son of the woman who owned the house became ill. He grew worse and worse, and finally stopped breathing. 18 She said to Elijah, "What do you have against me, man of God? Did you come to remind me of my sin and kill my son?"

19 "Give me your son," Elijah replied. He took him from her arms, carried him to the upper room where he was staying, and laid him on his bed. 20 Then he cried out to the LORD, "LORD my God, have you brought tragedy even on this widow I am staying with, by causing her son to die?" 21 Then he stretched himself out on the boy three times and cried out to the LORD, "LORD my God, let this boy's life return to him!"

22 The LORD heard Elijah's cry, and the boy's life returned to him, and he lived. 23 Elijah picked up the child and carried him down from the room into the house. He gave him to his mother and said, "Look, your son is alive!"

24 Then the woman said to Elijah, "Now I know that you are a man of God and that the word of the LORD from your mouth is the truth."

Turn to the person next to you and take turns sharing your answers to the following questions:

What was one thing that stood out to you from the reading?

What does this story have to say about the way God provides for us when we are in need?

Watch the Video

Play the video segment for Session 6. As you watch, use the following outline to record any thoughts or concepts that stand out to you.

Notes
The reality is that our situation may not resolve in this life. But there is still a promise and a hope that God has a comeback for us.

If we're honest with ourselves, we realize there are areas in our lives where we won't receive a comeback in this earthly life. Where do we turn when there seems to be no comeback?

In the story of Elijah and the widow of Zarephath, we encounter a woman who is at the end of a difficult life. She tells Elijah she has just enough flour to make one last meal for herself and her son. The story unfolds from the moment the woman decides to share that last meal with Elijah.

The overarching theme is not that life always works out the way we want, but that no matter how our stories ultimately turn out, Jesus is always enough.

God draws near to the brokenhearted and he saves those who are crushed in spirit. Even when we can't comprehend why things happen, we can still cling to the miracle of his presence.

All of our stories don't resolve in an instant. Sometimes it's just the promise that God is with us in the storm.

Sometimes, God will strip away the things we love the most, and strip away the things we lean on the most, so we can discover again that he really is all we need.

When the storms come and the torrent rages against us, we truly discover just how firm a foundation Jesus is beneath us. He is enough.

Group Discussion

Take a few minutes with your group members to discuss what you just watched and explore these concepts in Scripture.

First Impressions

1. Before everyone shares in the large group, turn to one or two people next to you and finish this sentence: "After watching the video, one question I now have is . . . "

Community Reflection

2. What is an area in your life or the life of someone you know where an earthly comeback is not possible? What hope has this session provided?

3. We all seek to "understand" tragic events when they happen. Why do we possess such a strong "need to know"? To what can we cling even when that understanding doesn't come?

4. In what ways is it often easier to trust God when things are going badly than when everything is smooth sailing?

5. How has Jesus revealed to you that he is a firm foundation in the midst of the storm?

6. There is a moment when we must discover that no matter how our stories turn out, Jesus is enough. What does that mean to you?

7. Does "Jesus is enough" sound like good news or news that's too good to be true? Why?

Opening Up to the Comeback

For this activity, each participant will need a pen and his or her sealed envelope from Session 1. (Those participants not in Session 1 will need a blank piece of paper and an envelope.)

One of the goals of this study has been to encourage you to trust in God's work and promises. He wants to bring about a comeback in your life, and wherever that comeback is in the process, you can count on him to finish what he started. When we began this journey, you wrote on a piece of paper an answer to this question: *If God could change one thing in my life right now, what would I want that to be?* This was a prayer for a comeback.

In this session, your group leader will give you the letter you wrote during Session 1. Spend the next five to ten minutes alone. First, reread that letter. Then, using the other side of the paper (where you wrote "help"), reflect on how you have (or have not) seen God working to answer this prayer during the last five weeks. Feel free to include any gratitude or lamentation this reflection evokes.

If you did not write a letter during Session 1, write a comeback prayer now based on your experience in this study. What would you like to see God do in your life during the next six weeks after this study? Are there any dreams that have been dashed that you want God to redeem? Where do you need Jesus to be enough?

Once everyone in your group has finished their reflection, gather back together. Invite anyone who would like to share what God has done, or what they hope God will do, to do so. Use the following prompts to close out your group time for *The Comeback*:

- "Before going through this study, I used to think _____, but now I know_____."
- The best thing about this experience was _____. The most challenging thing was _____.
- If I could describe my comeback experience in one word, it would be: _____.

Closing Prayer

End the meeting by inviting the group to pray silently for the person on their left. Pray that this person will stay open to the comeback that Jesus is already working out in his or her life.

PERSONAL STUDY FOR THE COMING DAYS

Further explore the good news of *The Comeback* this week by engaging in any or all of the following activities. *Be sure to read the reflection questions after each activity and make a few notes in your guide about the experience.* Consider sharing your reflections with a fellow group member or close friend sometime soon.

Action: Join the Divine Economy

This final session of *The Comeback* focuses on the economy of the kingdom of God. God's kingdom is one where nobody gets what they deserve, and everybody gets what they need. Yet trusting this truth can be tricky. When life throws us a curve ball, it ramps up our anxiety. What if we are not okay? What if we will not have what we need? What if it *is* really all up to us, and God can't be trusted? The final *Action* exercise of our study works in an opposite spirit of all this worry. You are invited to participate as a *giver* in God's divine economy.

Once or twice this week, act generously toward a stranger who is not expecting it. This can be anything from buying a cup of coffee for the person behind you at the drive-thru, to paying for the lunch of a person you don't know, to making a surprise donation to a charity, to anonymously slipping a grocery gift certificate into a coworker's mailbox.

Whatever you choose, make it something financial. Our biggest anxieties usually swirl around our money. So when you act generously this week, it can serve as a reminder that, in the same way the people you helped were not expecting it, there can also be blessing waiting for you when you least expect it. That's God's promise. He will take care of you, and when you join in the divine economy, you start to trust it for yourself.

Make a few notes about your experience to share with someone.

When Jesus is enough, we might be like the widow of Zarephath. The brook has run dry. The crops have failed. The oil and flour are gone. We have nothing left, and our hope is gone. All we can do now is eat a last meal and then die. If that's your story, you can rest assured Jesus is extending a huge invitation to you: give him your all. If Jesus is your all, and if Jesus is all you have left, then that's what it means that Jesus is enough.

—The Comeback, *page 158*

Contemplation: There Is Enough

For this week's contemplation, read the story of Jesus feeding the multitudes in Matthew 15:29–39:

> [29] *Jesus left there and went along the Sea of Galilee. Then he went up on a mountainside and sat down.* [30] *Great crowds came to him, bringing the lame, the blind, the crippled, the mute and many others, and laid them at his feet; and he healed them.* [31] *The people were amazed when they saw the mute speaking, the crippled made well, the lame walking and the blind seeing. And they praised the God of Israel.*
>
> [32] *Jesus called his disciples to him and said, "I have compassion for these people; they have already been with me three days and have nothing to eat. I do not want to send them away hungry, or they may collapse on the way."*
>
> [33] *His disciples answered, "Where could we get enough bread in this remote place to feed such a crowd?"*
>
> [34] *"How many loaves do you have?" Jesus asked.*
>
> *"Seven," they replied, "and a few small fish."*
>
> [35] *He told the crowd to sit down on the ground.* [36] *Then he took the seven loaves and the fish, and when he had given thanks, he broke them and gave them to the disciples, and they in turn to the people.* [37] *They all ate and were satisfied. Afterward the disciples picked up seven basketfuls of broken pieces that were left over.* [38] *The number of those who ate was four thousand men, besides women and children.* [39] *After Jesus had sent the crowd away, he got into the boat and went to the vicinity of Magadan.*

There is a popular meme on the Internet with a picture of a glass of water filled to the halfway point. The caption says,

"Is the cup half full or half empty? Neither. It is completely full of both water and air." This is a clever play on a popular adage that flips convention on its head. The cup is not half full or half empty because, in fact, it has been completely full the whole time.

In the story told in Matthew 15, Jesus and his disciples were out in a remote area. A large crowd had followed them there because Jesus was healing the sick, lame, and mute. Then Jesus called his disciples and said, "I have compassion for these people; they have already been with me three days and have nothing to eat. I do not want to send them away hungry, or they may collapse on the way." His disciples must have been in disbelief. This was a huge crowd, and they were nowhere near anyplace that could accommodate their needs. What did Jesus expect from them?

The disciples answered, "Where could we get enough bread in this remote place to feed such a crowd?" This was a reasonable and realistic question; it recognized the facts. There was no way they could see all those mouths getting fed. Jesus did not chastise them or engage them in a logistical debate about feeding this large group. He just asked, "How many loaves do you have?" We know what happens next.

When faced with a seemingly hopeless scenario, Jesus' first question was basically, "What have you already got?" This is monumental, because it shows that Jesus sees the world in a fundamentally different way than we do. For Jesus, there is enough. Period. He does not worry. He does not imagine an economy of scarcity where there are limited resources. Instead, Jesus sees a world where the cup has always been full.

Can you see the world this way too?

That is the question Matthew asks us, and it is the one we are challenged to consider when it comes to our own lives. Is there enough for us? Can Jesus meet our needs, even if we cannot see a way out? When we ask Jesus how any kind of comeback is possible, we need to allow him to ask us, "What do you already have?"

Then we can trust that with Jesus, there is already enough.

Are you more of a glass-half-full or glass-half-empty kind of person?

Where do you most find yourself worrying there will not be enough?

When it comes to the world's biggest problems, how can offering Jesus what you have be part of God's solution?

God often meets us most powerfully when we are willing to admit that we don't have the resources to move past the moment we're in. There is no Plan B. We have no strength left. We've run out of all human options. That's where the miracle happens. That's the comeback for us when we have no comeback. Jesus supplies us with what we need for the moment, for the day, for the season. And then he provides another grace after that and another grace after that. Grace isn't a one-time deposit. It's a moment-by-moment relationship with God, where we trust Jesus to be in us and through us and for us. We trust that he will come through in his own time and in his own way. When we have no comeback, the comeback is that Jesus is enough.

—The Comeback, *pages 160*

Reflection: Jesus Is Enough

Read Chapter 9 in *The Comeback* and reflect on the following questions:

- In what ways were you able to relate to Courtney as you read her story? What are some things in your life that you know *can't* come back? How have you dealt with that loss?
- How did Courtney discover that "Jesus is enough"? What type of grace does God offer to us in times of intense loss?
- In the story of the widow of Zarephath told in 1 Kings 17:8–24, why do you think God sent Elijah to get food from a woman in such poverty? What does this tell us about the way God's provision works? What similarities

are there between this story and Jesus feeding the five thousand in John 6:1–14?

- What does it say about the widow that she was willing to share her last meal with the prophet Elijah? What can we learn from her example about trusting God with our resources, giving all we have to him, and stepping out in faith?

- What does the phrase "Jesus is enough" mean to you in terms of your everyday life? What becomes our focus when we adopt this mindset? What does it compel us to do?

The ultimate comeback is Jesus Christ, the God-man, walking free from the jaws of death to give us our comebacks. This God always loves us, always cares for us, always offers us mercy and grace. He knows the big picture of everything, and he knows how our lives fit into that big picture. This is the God we're called to love and serve and follow today. Will you ask him that one question, the same question asked by the thief on the cross, the question you already know the answer to: Jesus, will you remember me today? That's how your comeback begins.

—The Comeback, *page 221*

ADDITIONAL RESOURCES FOR GROUP LEADERS

If you are reading this, you have likely agreed to lead a *Comeback* group study. Thank you! What you have chosen to do is important, and much good fruit can come from studies like this. Thanks again for sharing your time and talent.

The Comeback experience is as a six-session study built around video content and small group interaction. As the group leader, imagine yourself as the host of a dinner party. Your job is to take care of your guests by managing all the behind-the-scenes details so that as your guests arrive, they can focus on each other and on interaction around the topic.

As the group leader, your role is not to answer all the questions or reteach the content—the video, book, and study guide will do most of that work. Your job is to guide the experience and cultivate your small group into a kind of teaching community. This will make it a place for members to process, question, and reflect—not receive more instruction.

As such, make sure everyone in the group gets a copy of this study guide. Encourage them to write in their guide and bring it with them every week. This will keep everyone on the same page and help the process run more smoothly. Likewise, encourage each participant (or couple) to get a copy of the *The Comeback* book so they can complete the suggested readings in the *Reflection* sections. If this is not possible, see if anyone from the group is willing to donate an extra copy or two of the book for sharing. Giving everyone access to all the material will position this study to be as rewarding an experience as possible.

Hospitality

As group leader, you'll want to create an environment conducive to sharing and learning. A church sanctuary or formal classroom may not be ideal for this kind of meeting because those venues can feel formal and less intimate. Wherever you choose, make sure there is enough comfortable seating for everyone and, if possible, arrange the seats in a semicircle so everyone can see the video easily. This will make the transition from the video to group conversation more efficient and natural.

Also, try to get to the meeting site early so you can greet participants as they arrive, especially newcomers. Simple refreshments create a welcoming atmosphere and can be a wonderful addition to a group study gathering. If you do serve food, try to take into account any food allergies or dietary restrictions your group members may have. Also, if you meet in a home, find out if the house has pets (in case there are any allergies), and even consider offering childcare to couples with children who want to attend.

Finally, be sure your media technology is working properly. Managing these details up front will make the rest of your group experience flow effectively and provide a welcoming space in which to engage the content of *The Comeback*.

Leading Your Group

Once everyone has arrived, it will be time to begin the group. If you are new to leading small groups, what follows are some simple tips to make your group time healthy, enjoyable, and effective.

First, consider beginning the meeting with a word of prayer, and remind people to silence and put away their mobile phones. This is a way to say yes to being present to each other and to God.

Next, invite someone to read the session's "Orientation" from this study guide. This will get everyone on the same page regarding that week's topic. After the "Welcome and Checking In" time, your group will engage in a simple Bible study drawn from video content called "Hearing the Word." You do not need to be a biblical scholar to lead this effectively. Your role is only to open up conversation by using the instructions provided and to invite the group into the text.

Now that the group is fully engaged, it is time to watch the video. The content of each session from Louie Giglio is inspiring and challenging, so there is built-in time for personal reflection before anyone is asked to respond. Don't skip over this part. Internal processors will need more intimate space to sort through their thoughts and questions, and it will make the "Community Reflection" time more fruitful.

During the group discussion time, encourage everyone to participate, but make sure those who do not want to share (especially as the questions become more personal) know they do not have to do so. As the discussion progresses, follow up with questions such as, "Tell me more about that," or, "Why did you answer the way you did?" This will allow participants to deepen their reflections, and it invites meaningful sharing in a nonthreatening way.

You have been given multiple questions to use in each session. You do not have to use them all or follow them in order. Feel free to pick and choose questions based on either the needs of your group or how the conversation is flowing. Also, don't be afraid of silence. Offering a question and allowing up to thirty seconds of silence gives people space to think about how they want to respond and also gives them time to do so.

As group leader, you are the boundary keeper for your group. Do not let anyone (yourself included) dominate the discussion. Keep an eye out for group members who might be tempted to "attack" folks they disagree with or who try to "fix" those having struggles. Such behaviors can derail a group's momentum, so you need to discourage them from taking place. Model active listening and encourage everyone in your group to do the same. This will make your group time a safe space and foster the kind of community God can use to change people.

The "Community Reflection" time that follows the video leads to the final and most dynamic part of this study: "Opening Up to the Comeback." During this time, participants are invited to transform what they have learned into practical action. However, for this to be successful will require some preparation on your part. Take time to read each session's "Opening Up to the Comeback" segment, as several of them require special materials. Reading ahead will allow you to ask group members to bring any items you need but don't have, and it will give you a sense of how to lead your group through these experiences. Use the supply list below to make sure you have what you need for each session.

Supply List

Session 1
- Pens (one for each group member)
- Blank pieces of paper (one for each group member)
- Envelopes (one for each group member)

Session 2
- One bucket or pitcher, filled three-fourths full of water (pick a container that can sustain the impact of the rocks being dropped into it)
- Small decorating stones, pebbles, or river rocks (one for each group member)
- A low table for the supplies to sit on during the exercise

Session 3
- One candle for each group member
- Lighter or matches (to light the candles)
- A table or designated area for people to place their candles

Session 4
- Pens (one for each group member)
- Blank pieces of paper (one for each group member)

Session 5
- Compass (or compass app on a smart phone)

Session 6
- The letters each group member wrote to themselves during Session 1
- Pens (one for each group member)
- Blank piece of paper and an envelope (for anyone who was not part of Session 1)

Finally, even though instructions are provided for how to conclude each session, feel free to strike out on your own. Just make sure you do something intentional to mark the end of the meeting. It may also be helpful to take time before or after the closing prayer to go over that week's between-sessions activities, ask the group members which they would like to try, and answer any questions they have so everyone can depart in confidence.

Debriefing the Between-Sessions Materials

As just noted, each session includes an on-your-own section where everyone is invited to choose one or more of the activities to complete. Your job is to help group members debrief these experiences during the next session's "Welcome and Checking In" time.

Debriefing these activities is a bit different from responding to a video because the content comes from the participants' real lives. Though you are free to direct this time as you prefer, the basic experiences you want the group to reflect on are as follows:

- What was the best thing about the activity?
- What was the hardest thing about it?
- What did you learn about yourself?
- What did you learn about God?

Thank you again for taking the time to lead your group. May God reward your efforts and dedication and make your time together in *The Comeback* fruitful for his kingdom.